SMALL-GROU

FOR THE LOVE OF GOD +−

How the church is better and worse than you ever imagined

MARK STEPHENS   **JOHN DICKSON**   **SCOTT PETTY**

CENTRE
FOR
PUBLIC
CHRISTIANITY

Centre for Public Christianity

ACN 127 775 973

GPO Box 4161

Sydney NSW 2001

Australia

www.publicchristianity.org

ISBN: 978-0-647-53088-7

 A catalogue record for this
book is available from the
National Library of Australia

Mark Stephens, John Dickson, and Scott Petty assert their right under section 193 of the *Copyright Act 1968* (Cth) to be identified as the authors of this work.

Scripture quotations are taken from the Holy Bible, NEW INTERNATIONAL VERSION®, NIV® Copyright © 1973, 1978, 1984, 2011 by Biblica, Inc.® Used by permission. All rights reserved worldwide. NEW INTERNATIONAL VERSION® and NIV® are registered trademarks of Biblica, Inc. Use of either trademark for the offering of goods or services requires the prior written consent of Biblica US, Inc.

Editor: Kristin Argall

Cover layout: John Healy

Typesetting: John Healy

SESSIONS

The videos referred to in this
study guide can be found at

www.betterandworse.film

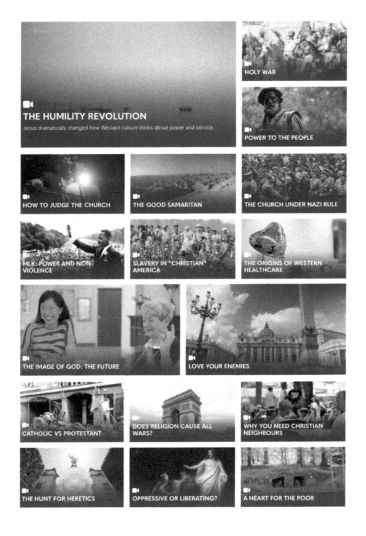

SESSION 1 **WAR + PEACE**

PART ONE

Introduction *(8 minutes)*[1]

Facilitator introduction

Welcome to *For the Love of God: How the church is better and worse than you ever imagined.*

The purpose of this short course is to explore the achievements and failures of the Christian church throughout its history, so that you can make up your own mind about the ongoing impact of Christianity in the modern world.

One key question frames this entire course:

How faithful has the church been to Jesus and his message?

To help us think this through, we are going to repeatedly draw upon a musical analogy. There have been many great compositions created through the ages. But no matter how beautifully written a piece of music, it can still be performed in a terrible way.

 Watch "How to Judge the Church: A Musical Analogy" *(3 minutes)*

This study assumes that Jesus gave the world a beautiful tune:

Love your enemies.
Do good to those who hate you.

---

[1] Throughout this guidebook, we will give time indications in brackets. They are suggestions only, provided to assist with completing each study in about an hour.

So, as we briefly survey the story of Christianity, we want to ask where the church has played "in tune" with Jesus, and consider those moments when the church has caused great harm by performing "out of tune."

Course orientation *(3 minutes)*

There are three simple things to keep in mind throughout the course:

- **Broad Christianity.** We use the word "Christianity" in its broadest sense. We are not promoting (or criticising) any particular brand of the Christian faith. For the purposes of this course, all the mainstream churches are representatives – for better or worse – of Jesus Christ.

- **Open Discussion.** Our questions are only meant to start a conversation, and you are encouraged to bring your own questions, experiences, and ideas.

- **The Bible.** The aim of the course is to examine the performance of the church against the backdrop of the teaching of the Bible, and especially the life and teaching of Jesus of Nazareth. Be assured: the course material assumes no prior knowledge of the Bible, and groups are free to work out what level of biblical study suits them.

Throughout all of these studies, we will regularly refer to the accompanying book to the documentary: Natasha Moore, John Dickson, Simon Smart, and Justine Toh, *For the Love of God: How the church is better and worse than you ever imagined* (Sydney: Centre for Public Christianity, 2019). This book provides helpful details to answer all of your additional questions. From this point onwards we will abbreviate this title with the acronym *FTLOG*.

 Starter question *(5 minutes)*

If you feel comfortable, introduce yourself to the group. Perhaps you might like to answer three questions:

1. What is your name?

2. What do you love doing during the week?

3. What would you like to learn from this course?

But what about the Crusades?

When discussing the impact of Christianity upon the world, the Crusades is often first in line as a negative example. So, let's begin there.

 Watch "Holy War: The Crusades" *(8 minutes)*

 Discussion *(15 minutes)*

1. What are your initial impressions from this clip?

   a. Was there anything that surprised you?

   b. Was there anything that was unclear?

2. People sometimes say, "Religion is the cause of most wars!" What is it about religion that invites such criticism?

3. Are there ways that contemporary Christians can do evil in the misguided belief they are doing good?

History can both horrify and explain. In the case of the Crusades, understanding its history first horrifies us. Yet history also helps explain how religious authority can be abused by the powerful. Moreover, history reveals how everyday people can be convinced to do evil, even while thinking it is for the sake of good. For more on the Crusades see Moore et al., *FTLOG*, 11–20.

The Old Testament and violence

Three-quarters of the Christian Bible is the Old Testament (OT). While Christians usually focus attention on Jesus, the OT is often seen as a problem for believers and non-believers. One topic of concern is the presence of violent acts which seem to be approved by God.

 **Watch "A Genocidal God?
Violence in the Old Testament"** *(8 minutes)*

 Discussion *(15 minutes)*

1. Does the conquest of Canaan in the OT sound like just an earlier version of the Crusades?

2. Iain Provan says the OT is anti-heroic. Do you agree with his point, and how might this change the way you read OT stories?

3. What is your reaction to the view that there are many things in the OT that are not to be imitated?

The OT is a large library of books which takes time and skill to read and understand. For further discussion on this topic, see Moore et al., *FTLOG*, 74–77.

Extra resources for further study

 Watch "The Hunt for Heretics: The Spanish Inquisition" *(10 minutes)*

OR

 Watch "Catholic vs Protestant: The Troubles of Northern Ireland" *(6 minutes)*

For either video, ask these questions:

1. Was there anything that surprised you?

2. How much is religion to blame for these conflicts?

Watch "Does Religion Cause All Wars?" *(2 minutes)*

If the group would like to explore in more detail the claim that "Religion is the cause of all war," watch this video.

Further reading

Moore et al., *FTLOG*, chapters 1, 2, 8.

Other good resources include:

- Christopher J. H. Wright, *The God I Don't Understand: Reflections on Tough Questions of Faith* (Grand Rapids: Zondervan, 2008), chapters 4 and 5.

- Tremper Longman, *Confronting Old Testament Controversies: Pressing Questions about Evolution, Sexuality, History, and Violence* (Grand Rapids: Zondervan, 2019), chapter 3.

- Christopher Tyerman, *The Crusades: A Very Short Introduction* (Oxford: Oxford University Press, 2005).

- Meic Pearse, *The Gods of War: Is Religion the Primary Cause of Violent Conflict?* (Downers Grove: InterVarsity, 2007).

SESSION 2 **WAR + PEACE**

PART TWO

Introduction *(5 minutes)*

Let's briefly recap last week, and the central topic of these studies. Has the church played in tune with the message of Jesus?

1. What insights have remained with you from last week?

2. Have any of your thoughts changed or developed with more time?

Starter question *(5 minutes)*

"I love Jesus, but I hate the church."
What kinds of feelings and thoughts do you have about this statement?

The message of Jesus

Jesus is the central character in the Christian story, and he remains popular even amongst the non-religious. Yet many of us have taken little time to consider how the life and teachings of Jesus have influenced our society and culture.

Watch "Love Your Enemies: Jesus on Violence"
(6 minutes)

 Discussion *(15 minutes)*

1. Read Matthew 5:43–48. Why is this countercultural in both Jesus' time and our contemporary age?

2. Read Romans 12:9–18. This is from Paul, an early Christian leader (apostle). What does this tell you about the early Christian church?

3. In your experience, how well do you think the church still practises the ethics of Jesus?

The ethics of Jesus provoke the complicated question of whether Christians should ever be involved in war. If the group would like to investigate this, they could watch the video "Curbing Violence" or read Moore et al., *FTLOG*, pp. 184–189.

The example of Martin Luther King Jr

The ethics of Jesus has sometimes been characterised as an "impossible" ethic, even by some theologians. But others have believed and demonstrated what it is like to live a life in tune with his message.

Watch "MLK: Power and Non-violence"
(8 minutes)

 Discussion *(15 minutes)*

1. The speeches of Martin Luther King Jr (MLK) might be familiar, but our focus here is on how MLK played in tune with Jesus.

   a. Did anything surprise you?

   b. Was anything unclear?

2. "Christian faith, at its very heart, is about grace … Grace that gives without seeking in return, and grace that gives also in a situation of injury which we call forgiveness" (Miroslav Volf).

   a. How did MLK show his belief in grace?

   b. Is this a different understanding of grace than you have encountered before?

   For more on MLK and his achievements, see Moore et al., *FTLOG*, 182–84; 189–95.

Conclusion *(5 minutes)*

Jesus lived and taught a vision of life characterised by forgiveness, mercy, and grace – themes embodied in his own self-sacrificing death on a Roman cross. At many times, and in various terrible ways, those who have claimed to follow Christ have conducted their lives according to violence, hatred, and vengeance. These cannot be readily explained away. They are part of the horrible history of the church, which Christians must own. Nevertheless Jesus, and many others since, have pursued his ethic of love, exemplifying the words, "Be merciful, just as your Father is merciful."

Where do you think "enemy love" is hardest to practise today?

Extra resources for further study

 Watch "MLK: The March for Votes" *(8 minutes)*

In this video, which looks at the struggle for civil rights in the United States, Simon Smart comments: "Martin Luther King operated on the conviction that the ultimate victory had already been won by Jesus, and non-violence was part of following him, or 'bearing his cross.'" Discuss your feelings and thoughts in response.

Further reading

Moore et al., *FTLOG*, chapters 8, 14.

Other good resources include:

- Jemar Tisby, *The Color of Compromise: The Truth about the American Church's Complicity in Racism* (Grand Rapids: Zondervan, 2019).

- Preston Sprinkle, *Fight: A Christian Case for Nonviolence* (Colorado Springs: David C. Cook, 2013).

- Scott Rae, *Moral Choices: An Introduction to Ethics*, 4th edn (Grand Rapids: Zondervan, 2018), chapter 10.

SESSION 3 **RIGHTS + WRONGS**

PART ONE

Introduction *(5 minutes)*

Let's briefly recap last week, and the central topic of these studies. Has the church played in tune with the message of Jesus?

1. What questions have started to emerge over the first two weeks?

2. Have you changed your mind on any ideas?

Starter question *(5 minutes)*

Leaving aside any theology, how could we argue that all people deserve equal dignity and respect?

The image of God

For most of human history, and across most human cultures, individuals were valued using criteria such as their status at birth, their skills and capacities, and their usefulness to society. As a result, societies tended to honour the smart, talented, strong, or beautiful, and to discard the weak and useless.

Watch "The Image of God: The Concept" *(7 minutes)*

 Discussion *(15 minutes)*

1. What are your initial impressions from this clip? Was there anything that surprised you? Was anything unclear?

2. Nick Spencer speaks about looking in the mirror each morning and seeing "a someone rather than a something." How do you think this idea has influenced our modern world?

3. Read Genesis 1:24–28. How does this text provide a grounding for the intuitive sense that we all have intrinsic value?

 Watch "The Genesis of Human Rights" *(7 minutes)*

 Discussion *(5 minutes)*

1. Some participants may be surprised or even sceptical that the concept of human rights has not been universal throughout history. Encourage participants to share their questions and concerns.

Watch "The Image of God: The Future" *(4 minutes)*

 Discussion *(10 minutes)*

"Christianity has taken the side of everything weak, base, ill-constituted ... Christianity is called the religion of compassion ... One loses force when one has compassion ... Compassion, on the whole, thwarts the law of evolution, which is the law of selection. It preserves that which is ripe for destruction; it defends life's disinherited and condemned ... In every noble morality it counts as weakness ... Nothing in our unhealthy modernity is more unhealthy than Christian compassion" (Friedrich Nietzsche).[1]

1. What is your response to the thoughts of 19th-century philosopher, Friedrich Nietzsche?

2. You don't have to believe in God to treat people with dignity, but are there dangers if society drifts from the Christian idea of the value of life?

3. Where do you see evidence in the contemporary world of the weak, powerless, and disinherited being ignored or even destroyed?

---

[1] Adapted from Friedrich Nietzsche, *Twilight of the Idols/The Anti-Christ*, trans. by R. J. Hollingdale, (Penguin: London, 1968), 117–119. We have here taken the liberty of re-translating as "compassion" the term that appears in the original passage as "pity", the latter English term having shifted in meaning over the last century from the kinds of positive sympathy with the plight of others that we now associate with "compassion" to acquire more negative connotations, as something condescending and undesirable.

The idea of the image of God seems normal to us today, but in the context of the ancient world it is the expansion of this honour to all people that is truly radical. In the modern world, too, it has been far from the norm to see everyone as worthy of dignity and respect. For more discussion of the image of God, and its relationship to modern discussion of human rights, see Moore et al., *FTLOG*, 172–81.

Conclusion *(5 minutes)*

Throughout this course we are examining how well the church has performed the "tune" of Jesus.

Regarding human dignity, Jesus tells a famous story, often called the Parable of the Prodigal Son, to illustrate the way God thinks about all human beings, even those who disobey him. According to Jesus, even those who do not live as God's image-bearers are still regarded by God as his children – disobedient children, but children nonetheless – who are being called to turn around and be welcomed home.

Read Luke 15:11–32 as a closing reflection.

Extra resources for further study

 Watch "Power to the People: Luther, Tyndale, and the Road to Democracy" *(8 minutes)*

This video looks at how the image of God influenced the English and German languages. After viewing, ask these questions:

1. Why does Bible translation tell us something about how we think about people?

2. How do these ideas shape our understanding of education and democracy?

Further reading

Moore et al., *FTLOG*, chapter 13.

Other good resources include:

- Nick Spencer, *The Evolution of the West: How Christianity has Shaped our Values* (London: SPCK, 2016), 51–63, 125–137.

- Jonathan Hill, *What Has Christianity Ever Done for Us? Its Role in Shaping the World Today* (Oxford: Lion, 2005).

- John F Kilner (ed.), *Why People Matter: A Christian Engagement with Rival Views of Human Significance* (Grand Rapids: Baker Academic, 2017).

- David P. Gushee, *The Sacredness of Human Life: Why an Ancient Biblical Vision is Key to the World's Future* (Grand Rapids: Eerdmans, 2013).

SESSION 4 **RIGHTS + WRONGS**

PART TWO

Introduction *(5 minutes)*

Let's briefly recap last week, and the ideas of the image of God and human dignity.

1. What surprised you, if anything, about last week's study?

2. What questions remain?

 Starter question *(5 minutes)*

"The Bible supports slavery." Discuss.

But what about slavery?

The idea of the image of God sounds beautiful in theory. But the record of the church in treating every person with equal dignity is decidedly mixed. Perhaps there is no bigger example than that of slavery. If we are going to be honest about the impact of Christians upon the world, both the good and the bad need to be acknowledged.

Watch "Slavery in Christian America" *(9 minutes)*

 Discussion *(10 minutes)*

1. How does this clip make you feel?

2. What role did the Bible play for both slaveholders and for slaves?

 Watch "Am I Not a Man and a Brother?" *(8 minutes)*

 Discussion *(10 minutes)*

1. Why was slavery so hard to challenge?

2. How can some people use the Bible to justify slavery while others use it to abolish slavery?

The campaign to end the transatlantic slave trade is rightly celebrated as a triumph of patient and persistent Christian influence on a culture. Yet it was no overnight success. If we just consider Wilberforce's involvement with the abolitionist movement, it required twenty years of parliamentary effort before the slave trade was made illegal. It was another twenty-six years before slavery was outlawed altogether. For more on Wilberforce, see Moore et al., *FTLOG*, 73–79.

The New Testament and slavery

Did early Christians endorse slavery? *(15 minutes)*

Slavery is based on denying people dignity and treating them as property. It is the very antithesis of treating all people as God's image-bearers. But the New Testament was written to a world where slavery was widespread and assumed. In addition, the early Christians had no political power in the Roman Empire, and they did not try to overthrow the institution. So, what did they do?

 Watch "The Image of God: The Impact" *(5 minutes)*

Read Ephesians 6:5–9

1. How does this text subvert the general attitudes to slaves in the 1st century?

2. Including the comments provided in the video, how did the approach of the early Christians ultimately prove effective in undermining slavery?

Christians throughout history have often sought to "make the best of it" (John Stackhouse). When it came to their attitude to slavery, they did what they could with what they had. This might seem feeble to us, but it flowed out of the "image of God" ideal, and it ignited a "long fuse of argument and discovery" (Rowan Williams) that changed things like the abandoning of children on rubbish dumps and the widespread use of slavery in the ancient world. For more on this issue see Moore et al., *FTLOG*, 48–59.

Conclusion

Break into groups of two or three. Role-play a conversation starting with the following statement:

"Christians should stay quiet on politics and social issues because the Bible was used to support slavery"

How would you respond?

Further reading

Moore et al., *FTLOG*, chapter 5.

Other good resources include:

- Heather Andrew Williams, *American Slavery: A Very Short Introduction* (Oxford: Oxford University Press, 2014).

- Paul Copan, *Is God a Moral Monster? Making Sense of the Old Testament God* (Grand Rapids: Baker, 2011), chapters 12–14.

- Peter J. Williams, "Does the Bible Support Slavery?", https://www.bethinking.org/bible/does-the-bible-support-slavery.

SESSION 5 **RICH + POOR**

PART ONE

Introduction *(5 minutes)*

We are repeatedly asking the question, how well has the church played in tune with Jesus? Now we get to a topic that *regularly* pops up in conversation: the church and money.

 Let's begin with a discussion starter:
1. "The church is only interested in money for itself." Discuss.

Filthy lucre

In Western countries, we can still see examples where Christian institutions, including the church, are in possession of great power and wealth. This raises questions about how power is acquired, and how such wealth continues to be used.

 Watch "Treasures on Earth" *(5 minutes)*

 Discussion *(10 minutes)*

1. Was there anything in this clip which was surprising or unclear?

2. In your opinion, why did some people in the church turn the message of Jesus into an opportunity for profit?

3. Could the same criticisms be made of churches today?

My money and my neighbour

The topic of money is part of the tune of Jesus. Indeed, in the Gospels of Matthew, Mark, and Luke, Jesus speaks of money just as much as he speaks of love. Yet the message Jesus brings is one that is both surprising and shocking, both in his world and in ours.

 Watch "The Good Samaritan" *(5 minutes)*

 Discussion *(15 minutes)*

Read Luke 10:25–37

1. Why does a story like the Good Samaritan push beyond conventional notions of charity?

2. The expert in the law asks Jesus, "Who is my neighbour?" Does Jesus answer his question?

3. "The best kind of care that the church has provided for the world has been when it's out of power and it's not worried about ruling but

more worried about being on the ground, taking care of the poor and the vulnerable" (William Cavanaugh). Do you agree? How might this challenge the public actions of Christians?

Go and do likewise

The New Testament scholar Klyne Snodgrass says that "love does not allow limits on the definition of neighbor."[1] This sounds like a noble ideal, or a beautiful tune – to use the image that has framed these studies. Have you seen or experienced concrete examples of that "tune" being played well? What has been the result of such action?

 Watch "The Origins of Western Healthcare" *(7 minutes)*

 Discussion *(10 minutes)*

1. Some thinkers, like the German philosopher Friedrich Nietzsche, recommended that the healthy should avoid any association with the sick and the weak. Do you think this attitude is still present today?

2. How does the Christian response to illness inspire you?

---

[1] Klyne R. Snodgrass, *Stories with Intent: A Comprehensive Guide to the Parables of Jesus* (Grand Rapids: Eerdmans, 2008), 357.

Conclusion *(5 minutes)*

From this study, write down one specific insight you have learned, and one specific response you might make.

Extra resources for further study

 Watch "The Leper Priest: Father Damien of Molokai" *(5 minutes)*

After viewing, discuss the following question:

1. How does the example of Father Damien exemplify that love does not put limits on who is my neighbour?

Further reading

Moore et al., *FTLOG*, chapters 3, 4, and 15.

Other good resources include:

- Nick Spencer, *The Evolution of the West* (London: SPCK, 2016), 167–184.

- Tom Holland, *Dominion: The Making of the Western Mind* (London: Little, Brown, 2019), 119–141.

SESSION 6 **RICH + POOR**

PART TWO

Introduction *(5 minutes)*

This is our second week on the topic of money and the church. Last week, we encountered the mixed influence of the church. This week we look at the specific question of charity towards the poor.

Let's begin with another discussion starter:

1. What is your attitude towards giving money to the poor? What shapes your decision on who you might support?

Looking after your own

Sometimes we can think that ideas and morals have remained consistent across the ages. We assume the basic template for being a good person was the same in the ancient world as it is in the modern world. But the idea of sharing wealth with others looked very different in the past. This helps us appreciate how the message of Jesus would have been understood in his time.

 Watch "Being Poor in the Ancient World" *(8 minutes)*

 Discussion *(15 minutes)*

1. What guided generosity in the ancient world according to the examples given in the clip?

2. The video refers to the love of honour as a motivation for ancient giving. How is this different from true charity? Does love of honour remain a motivation today?

3. Read Luke 14:34–36. In what ways do these commands of Jesus contrast with the classical world?

Freely you have received, freely give

The Christian story has God's grace at its centre, where God acts to love and forgive people who have not earned his love. This belief changes everything about how we think human beings should relate to God, but it also transforms how human beings might relate to each other.

 Watch "The Invention of Charity: Jews, Christians, and the God of the Poor" *(7 minutes)*

 Discussion *(15 minutes)*

Read Deuteronomy 24:19–22 and Ephesians 4:28

1. How does it change our perspective on wealth to see it as a gift we steward rather than something that we own?

2. Why was the charity of Jews and Christians different to other types of "giving" in the ancient world?

3. The Emperor Julian once complained about the generosity of Christians. Would the same complaint be made today?

Conclusion

We started last week looking at examples of obscene wealth in the history of the church (see the clip "Treasures on Earth").

To conclude this week's study, let's look at another example – one that is much more in tune with the message of Jesus.

 Watch "A Heart for the Poor: The 7th Earl of Shaftesbury" *(5 minutes)*

As a final discussion topic, have the group share whether Christians today are known for their generosity to the poor.

Extra resources for further study

 Watch "Why You Need Christian Neighbours: Faith and Social Capital" *(6 minutes)*

Once the video has finished, discuss the following question:

1. "If Christianity is true then it ought to follow … that any Christian will be nicer than the same person would be if he were not a Christian" (C. S. Lewis).[1] In light of the video clip, do you agree?

---

[1] C. S. Lewis, *Mere Christianity* (New York: Macmillan, 1952), 177.

Further reading

Moore et al., *FTLOG*, chapters 4, 16, and 17

Other good resources include:

- Rodney Stark, *The Triumph of Christianity: How the Jesus Movement Became the World's Largest Religion* (New York: HarperOne, 2011), 105–120.

- Alan Kreider, *The Patient Ferment of the Early Church* (Grand Rapids: Baker, 2016), 91–132.

SESSION 7 **POWER + HUMILITY**

PART ONE

Introduction *(5 minutes)*

This series of studies has considered past occasions when the church used its power, both for good and for ill. We now live in a time of declining social influence for the church.

1. Why do you think the power of the church has declined?

2. Is this a good thing?

It's all Constantine's fault

Most of us are vaguely aware that somehow Christianity went from being a persecuted minority to a favoured religion. We don't need to unpack all of that complicated history, but it is helpful for us to consider some key events which changed the status and power of Christian believers.

 Watch "The Empire Converts" *(5 minutes)*

 Discussion *(10 minutes)*

1. Do you see the conversion of the Roman emperor as mostly negative or mostly positive?

2. "Christian history is littered with instances of Christians behaving badly when they have the chance to pull the levers of power" (John Stackhouse). What is your response to this comment?

3. Should the church ever seek social and political power?

What about Hitler?

The 20th century witnessed some of the worst regimes in history. Some of these were atheistic, such as Stalinist Soviet Russia. But other regimes saw the church become complicit in the broader crimes perpetrated under their rule.

 Watch "The Church Under Nazi Rule" *(5 minutes)*

 Discussion *(15 minutes)*

1. Did anything shock or surprise you about the story of the German church under Nazism?

2. "... not just to bandage the victims under the wheel, but to jam a spoke in the wheel itself" (Dietrich Bonhoeffer).[1] Do you agree? What might that mean today?

---

[1] Geffrey B. Kelly and F. Burton Nelson (eds), *A Testament to Freedom: The Essential Writings of Dietrich Bonhoeffer* (HarperOne: New York, 1995), 132.

3. How is Bonhoeffer's life relevant to us who live in less extreme circumstances?

Biblical reflection *(10 minutes)*

Read Mark 10:35–45.

1. What were James and John seeking that was so out of tune with Jesus?

2. What does this passage tells us about Jesus' expectations of his followers?

Conclusion

"The church is church only when it is there for others … not dominating, but helping and serving. It must tell people in every calling what a life with Christ is, what it means 'to be there for others'" (Dietrich Bonhoeffer).[2]

1. Share with each other your experiences of when the church has both succeeded and failed in this ideal.

2. Draw together the big themes that have emerged from your conversation throughout this session.

---

[2] Dietrich Bonhoeffer, *Letters and Papers from Prison*, trans. Isabel Best et al., Dietrich Bonhoeffer Works Volume 8 (Minneapolis: Fortress, 2010), 503.

Extra resources for further study

 Watch "The Colonial Project: Christianity in the Age of Empire" *(9 minutes)*

Discuss the following question after viewing:

1. What enabled some Christians to act against the racism of the colony, including their fellow churchgoers?

 Watch "Witches: Fear and Loathing in Salem" *(8 minutes)*

Discuss the following question after viewing:

1. The story of Salem is more complex than we first think. How should that affect the way we judge the actions of the church?

Further reading

Moore et al., *FTLOG*, chapters 7, 9.

Other good resources include:

- Dietrich Bonhoeffer, *The Cost of Discipleship* (London: SCM, 1964).

- John Harris, *One Blood: 200 Years of Aboriginal Encounter with Christianity*, 2nd edn (Sutherland: Albatross, 1994).

- Alan Kreider, *The Patient Ferment of the Early Church: The Improbable Rise of Christianity in the Roman Empire* (Grand Rapids: Baker Academic, 2016).

SESSION 8 **POWER + HUMILITY**

PART TWO

Introduction *(5 minutes)*

We began this course with the purpose of exploring the achievements and failures of the Christian church throughout its history. As we prepare for this final study, let's voice our conclusions so far, through answering this question:

1. What good has Christianity been for the world?

The missionaries ruined everything

Christian churches often celebrate the life and work of crosscultural missionaries who take the gospel to distant lands. At the same time, many movies, documentaries, and newspaper articles assume that missionaries were mere agents of colonialism, who destroyed the idyllic lives of native peoples and their culture.

 Watch "How Missionaries Changed the World"
(9 minutes)

 Discussion *(15 minutes)*

1. Were you surprised that research has pointed to positive impacts of missionary influence? Why/why not?

2. Why might education and social renewal go together with the Christian message?

3. What drove people like William Carey and the Serampore Trio to do what they did?

The humility revolution

At the centre of William Carey's life was the practice of humility. Today, humility is seen as a virtuous and noble attitude to one's life and achievements. But the notion of humility as something worthy has a history, and exploring that story offers insight into how Jesus changed the world we know.

 Watch "The Humility Revolution" *(10 minutes)*

 Discussion *(15 minutes)*

1. Read Philippians 2:6–11. Why does the story of Jesus, and not just his teaching, challenge our attitude towards holding power?

2. From this New Testament passage, how would you distinguish "humility" from "being a doormat" for other people to walk over? What is the heart of humility?

3. The documentary points to material evidence that shows how humility changes the way people relate to one another. What kind of evidence would show an attitude of humility today?

Conclusion: Returning to the tune of Jesus

 Watch "The Tune of Jesus: Final Thoughts" *(1 minute)*

"When Christians have played out of tune with Jesus, the results have been disastrous … But when they've followed in his footsteps, and played the tune well, that's shaped our world in ways we can all be glad of" (Justine Toh and Simon Smart).

1. In what ways has your view of Christ and/or the church changed over the course of our eight sessions together?

2. What questions remain?

Extra resources for further study

 Watch "Oppressive or Liberating? Christianity and Women" *(6 minutes)*

The following are some suggested questions after watching this video:

1. What is your reaction to Rodney Stark's claim that "it's surprising that every woman in the Roman Empire didn't become a Christian overnight"?

35

2. Like many examples throughout this study, the record of the church towards women is mixed. Has the oppression of women hindered Christianity's ability to influence the world in positive ways?

Further reading

Moore et al., *FTLOG*, chapters 10, 11.

Other good resources include:

- John Dickson, *Humilitas: A Lost Key to Life, Love and Leadership* (Grand Rapids: Zondervan, 2011).

- Vishal Mangalwadi, *The Book that Made Your World: How the Bible Created the Soul of Western Civilisation* (Nashville: Thomas Nelson, 2011).